TEACHER'S MANUAL

Talk Your Head Off

(...and Write, Too!)

written by *Brana Rish West*

illustrated by *Harlan West*

PRENTICE HALL REGENTS

Upper Saddle River, New Jersey 07458

Publisher: *Louisa B. Hellegers*
Development Editor: *Barbara Barysh*
Production Editor: *Ken Liao*
Art Director: *Merle Krumper*

Compositor: *Harlan West Design*

Printed in the United States of America

ISBN 0-13-613605-2

10 11 12 13 14 15 OPM 09 08

Table of Contents

*Lesson number (also) indicates page number in *Teacher's Manual.*

Table of Contents

Table of Contents

Lesson Topic	Competency Objectives	Structures
17 **Stress** *Student Book pp. 65-68*	Express ideas on stress and ways of coping with it • Do a crossword puzzle • Listen to student's stressful situations	Adjective comparatives: *less than, more than*
18 **Moving Children Out** *Student Book pp. 69-72*	Discuss situations about adult children living at home • Talk about cultural differences on adult children moving out • Write a personal essay	*Say* and *tell* review
19 **Growing Old** *Student Book pp. 73-76*	Listen to a description • Discuss aging using personal and cultural ideas • Write an imaginative story	Pronunciation of past regular verbs
20 **Pollution and Recycling** *Student Book pp. 77-80*	Talk about environmental issues • Propose some solutions to problems • Create an environmental group	Passive voice
21 **The Homeless and Welfare** *Student Book pp. 81-84*	Discuss homelessness • Give opinions on welfare • Write an opinion letter	Use of *some* and *any*
22 **Disasters** *Student Book pp. 85-88*	Talk about disasters and their preventions	Introduction to future perfect
23 **Smoking** *Student Book pp. 89-92*	Express ideas on smoking • Talk about the right's of smokers and non-smokers • Write about hazards of smoking	*Could* as probability • *Should* review
24 **Gambling** *Student Book pp. 93-96*	Discuss views on gambling • Talk about effects on society • Talk about personal gambles • Write a personal essay	Use of *ever* in the present perfect review

Table of Contents

Table of Contents

To the Teacher

Talk Your Head Off is a conversation textbook for intermediate through advanced students of English as a second language. It can be used in a variety of settings, including adult education programs, language institutes, and universities. The goal of the book is to help students learn to communicate effectively in English.

The material in the book is based on a combination of pedagogical perspectives. From the behavioral perspective, the goal is for students to be able to converse effectively in English. Students demonstrate their success by speaking English. As they proceed through the text, they will notice a dramatic improvement not only in their speaking skills but also in their confidence and mastery of the language. The text frequently requires students to refer to their own life experiences, thereby incorporating the experiential perspective on education. Many questions involving deduction and critical thinking are included in the book, providing the basis for a cognitive perspective in the educational process.

Three main teaching techniques can be used in combination with the text: the direct method, the communicative approach, and suggestopedia. The direct method emphasizes practice in the target language only. Immersion methods in language teaching encourage early language production and retention. In the communicative approach, conversation utilizes authentic language. Since communication is a process, students apply the knowledge they learn in conversations to understanding the language. They learn language to communicate. Suggestopedia creates a completely positive and relaxed atmosphere as instructors suggest to students that they will be successful in their learning endeavor. Much attention is given to students' feelings. Students need to trust the teacher, to feel confident they can learn, and to be in as relaxed an atmosphere as possible. Posters of grammatical forms and relevant vocabulary are hung where students can see them and thereby acquire language through peripheral learning. (Instructors do not need to translate everything for students, even though the method of suggestopedia suggests it.) Most activities in the text incorporate the perspective and techniques mentioned, and they also have the students work cooperatively in groups or pairs. Since research shows that small-group and pair work increase the learning process dramatically, this text emphasizes interaction among students as an important step toward language acquisition.

This Teacher's Manual was written to make instructors' lesson preparation as simple as possible. The exercises in the student text are self-explanatory, so this manual does not repeat simple directions already given in the student book. Instead, the Teacher's Manual outlines each student text lesson by listing the vocabulary, irregular verb forms, grammar focus, and additional ideas for expanding on the lesson.

The *Vocabulary Section* lists all the topic-related vocabulary used for each lesson. All vocabulary is pertinent, so you should pronounce, define, and briefly explain all the words to the students. You can do this by using example sentences, pictures, pantomime, or role play. Encourage students to add their own relevant vocabulary to each lesson.

The *Irregular Verb Form* section contains only past verbs and past participles. The two irregular present tense verbs used in the text, *be* and *have*, should already be familiar to students at this level. You can teach irregular verb forms by giving students example sentences or by drilling practice with flashcards (with the base form on one side and the past and past participle on the other). Once the irregular verb forms are introduced it is necessary to practice them on a daily basis. In the back of this Teacher's Manual there are some games which provide students with the practice they need without the boredom of constant repetitive drills.

The next section in the Teacher's Manual is the *Grammar Focus*. Note that *Talk Your Head Off* implements a liberal and conversational grammatical structure in its lessons. Prepositions occur at the end of sentences because they rarely, if ever, occur at the beginning in spoken English. Contractions are used, because they are conversational, and they usually do not violate standard English rules.

To someone looking for grammar focus in the student text, the structure might not be immediately apparent. The structural foci in this book are carefully embedded in the lessons to encourage students to answer using the correct forms. Teachers act as facilitators to help students provide the forms. Many of the lessons demonstrate new grammatical experiences; however, all lessons incorporate previously introduced grammatical structures. Therefore, each lesson contains a multiplicity of grammatical forms. Furthermore, the book gradually increases in grammatical complexity from lesson to lesson. For this reason, it is best to follow the lessons in order. The idea is not to have students practice one grammatical form at a time, but rather to continue what they know while learning new structures.

With that in mind, the *Grammar Focus* section in this Teacher's Manual tries to give a clear yet simple explanation to the grammatical structures used in the text. Sometimes, in order to explain a grammatical structure, additional examples are given on those forms that might not be in the text. Further, the explanations are not in the intricate detail that would be found in a grammar book. The idea is to provide a basis for a grammatical explanation if the teacher desires to give one. (Some ESL teachers prefer a notional functional approach and don't teach grammar directly. This text works for either style of teaching.) If you are emphasizing grammatical structures, you can point out the particular forms to the students before they begin talking in their groups.

The *Expanding on the Lesson* section provides additional ideas that correspond to the lesson topic. Exercises, activities, and additional questions are given to broaden the conversational aspect of each topic. Additional relevant vocabulary words are boldfaced.

About the book

There are five sections to each lesson in the student text: *Vocabulary, Usage, Let's Start, Let's Talk*, and an *exercise and activities* page.

The *vocabulary* section is divided into *New Words* and *Let's Talk Words*. The *New Words* are the words on the first page of the lesson. They are used to acquaint the students with the topic. The *Let's Talk* words are also topic-related words and give students the vocabulary necessary to produce their own original sentences for the *Let's Talk* section.

The *Usage* section helps students become acquainted with the vocabulary words through matching, writing, defining and drawing exercises, as well as word association, short reading passages, and games. This section gives students practice using the vocabulary words they have just learned. The exercises are meant for group, pair, or class practice. The students help each other use and understand the meaning of the words through activities. The activities are eclectic to prevent boredom, and, at the same time, accommodate various learners' styles.

Let's Start provides activities that encourage students to get ready for conversing. Talking in groups or as a class, sharing ideas, using imagination, and speaking are the elements that compose this section.

To the Teacher

The *Let's Talk* section is the core of the text. To work in the *Let's Talk* section, students should be in groups of four to six. This section is filled with adult topics and questions. The topics increase in difficulty not only grammatically but also in social sensitivity. The questions in this section lead the students into forming original sentences that stem from their own experiences, opinions, and beliefs. There are no correct answers to the majority of the questions; however, they are written so that students should answer each question with a particular grammatical structure. As mentioned previously, although a new structure is introduced or reviewed in each lesson, a multiplicity of grammatical forms are used in all lessons.

"Real world" English involves a conglomeration of grammatical structures even within basic conversations. Students need to practice using as many grammatical sequences as possible in their conversations. Thus, it is important to let the students know that, unlike many books, in this book they will practice more than one grammatical structure in each lesson.

Finally, to close each lesson, there is an exercises and activities page where students take surveys, write their thoughts, and expand on the topics. The survey section encourages students to meet and converse with other students, gives additional practice in creative speaking and listening, and allows them to practice writing.

In *Talk Your Head Off*, well-known theories and methods are combined in the text to make acquiring the ability to speak proficiently in English as entertaining and as enjoyable as possible. We are confident that this combination of perspectives in education and methodologies in teaching, along with practical and interesting conversational topics, will significantly increase students' attention in class and thereby raise their learning capacity and level of proficient English conversation.

Acknowledgments

We would like to thank the people who helped develop and produce this book. We appreciate the dedicated teamwork of Prentice Hall Regents that helped us through the publishing process. Thank you, Arley Gray, for granting us the opportunity to work with your team of experts. We appreciate all the feedback and guidance we received from Louisa Hellegers, Ken Liao, and Sheryl Olinsky. We are especially grateful for the help of Barbara Barysh, our editor, who oversaw the complete process of the book from development through production. Without her dedication, expertise, and experience—coupled with kindness, encouragement, and guidance—this book would never have been published.

In addition we want to thank our family, friends, and colleagues for their unlimited enthusiasm, encouragement, and help. Thank you Paul Hamel, Mike Bennett, Jean Owensby, Marvin and Dorothy Rish, Alan West and Lois Fine, David Rish, Nathan Rish, Ethel Rish, Adam West, Stacie Steinberg, Wendy Rosenthal LeBlang, and Chagall and Cotton West.

Brana and Harlan West

This book is dedicated to the memory of Joyce West, a loving mother and teacher who inspired us to achieve.

Introductions

Vocabulary New Words

country	meet
do	month
have	name
how long	say
introduce	see
am	is
are	language
been	learn
	speak
	what
	where

Let's Talk Words

city	mark (check)
class	married
community	same as
different from	share
else	single
job	study
like	travel
live	visit

Irregular Verb Forms

Base Form	Past	Past Participle
be	was / were	been
do	did	done
have	had	had
meet	met	met
say	said	said
see	saw	seen
speak	spoke	spoken

Grammar Focus

Simple present

Use the simple present tense to show:

- Habitual actions in the present
  I meet new people every day. He speaks English all the time.

- Uses with stative verbs, especially *be*
  I am a teacher. He is a student. They are good workers.

- Present perceptions and emotions
  I like my job. She likes to travel. We like this class.

Present perfect

Use the present perfect to depict:

- A past action that continues to the present
  I have taken piano lessons for two years.

- A recently completed action
  I have just spoken to Bill about the report.

- A past experience or action with current relevance
  Please tell Dave I have already met Sally.

Expanding on the Lesson

After students have introduced themselves in the Name Tag Game, try variations of the game by having students state their occupations, their hobbies, the languages they speak, or their field of study.

Invite students to respond by asking the following questions:

How are introductions different . . .

- at work?
- at a **formal party**?
- at a **casual get-together**?
- made by a friend?

When is it **appropriate** to . . .

- **shake hands**?
- **hug**?
- smile and **make eye contact**?
- kiss?

Lesson 2

Favorite Things

Vocabulary

New Words

breakfast	lunch
child	meal
dinner	play
eat	sport
favorite	sporting event
go	thing
kind of	

Let's Talk Words

actor	put
actress	singer
ethnic	which
hobby	_____
player	_____
popular	_____
	_____

Irregular Verb Forms

Base Form	Past	Past Participle
eat	ate	eaten
go	went	gone
put	put	put

Grammar Focus

Questions: present/past/present perfect

To form a question:

- With the verb *be*, a modal, or the auxiliary *have*, invert the usual sentence order.
  Are they students? Is her name Jane? Have you gone to any restaurants this month?

- When there is no verb *be*, modal, or auxiliary, use the correct tense of the auxiliary *do* before the subject.
  Do they study every day? What radio station do you listen to?

- After the auxiliary *do*, use the base form of the verb (without *to*).
  What kind of music does he like? Did you go to the movies last month?

- When *who* or *what* is the subject, the auxiliary *do* is not used.
  Who watches TV with you in the evening? What happened after class?

Expanding on the Lesson

Have students work with a partner. Ask them to create **categories** for their favorite things. Have them list other items under each **category**. Then have students **brainstorm** as a class. (For example, if a student likes soccer, the category is sports. The pair of students lists as many sports as they can. The class then adds to their list of sports.)

Find out more about the class. Ask them these questions.

- What do you like to do in your free time?

- What are your favorite things to buy?

- What are your favorite school subjects? What kind of books do you like to read?

Have students talk about their favorite

- travel experiences.
- **amusement parks**, zoos, museums.
- **toys** they had when they were children.
- **childhood memories**.

- places to be alone.
- cities to visit.
- people to be with.
- relatives to talk to.

Lesson 3

Diet and Exercise

Vocabulary New Words

balanced diet	kick
dairy	leg
draw	meat
drink	snack
elbow	stand up
exercise (routine)	toe
fast food	touch
food	twist
fruit	vegetable
jump	vitamin
junk food	waist

Let's Talk Words

ankle	hand	perfect
arm	head	balance
back	if not	shoulder
become	if so	stay
bread	knee	stomach
certain	lose	take
diet	low fat	think
discuss	make	vegetarian
eye	neck	was
food group	nutritious food	weight
foot	overweight	were

Irregular Verb Forms

Base Form	Past	Past Participle
become	became	become
draw	drew	drawn
drink	drank	drunk
lose	lost	lost
make	made	made
stand	stood	stood
take	took	taken
think	thought	thought

Grammar Focus

Imperatives

Use the imperative to:

- Give an order
  Eat your vegetables! Don't jump on the bed!

- Give a direction
  Discuss your exercise routine. Turn right at the next light.

- Make a polite request
  Please eat lunch with us. Please eat some more food.

Expanding on the Lesson

Use The Total Physical Response method (TPR) to teach the body parts. Say the body part, touch it, and have students mimic what you tell them to do. Then play Simon Says as a class. To play Simon Says touch your head, for example, and say, "Simon says, touch your head." The students should touch their heads. If you give a command, but do not say "Simon says," the class does not follow the order. As Simon, you can try to trick the class by calling out one command and doing something else. If students don't follow the command, or follow an order without "Simon says" preceding it, they must sit down. The game ends when only one student is standing.

Have students write and discuss their favorite recipes. Make a class recipe book.

Ask the class these additional questions:

- What **diseases** can people avoid by eating a proper diet?

- Why is it important to exercise daily?

- How has public opinion on staying healthy changed?

Lesson 4 Transportation Systems

Vocabulary

bus
can
carpool
drive
fly

New Words

might
passenger
plane
ride
situation
train
transportation system
use
will

Let's Talk Words

encourage
environment
government
improve
native
subway
teleportation
world

_____
_____
_____
_____
_____
_____
_____
_____
_____

Irregular Verb Forms

Base Form	Past	Past Participle
drive	drove	driven
fly	flew	flown
ride	rode	ridden

Grammar Focus

Modals *can/will/might*

Use *can* (*can't*) to show:

- Ability
  He can drive. They can't fly an airplane.

- Permission in some questions
  Can I ride my bicycle now? Can Bobby have some cookies?

- Request in some questions
  Can you drive me to work tomorrow?

Use *will* (*won't*) to show:

- A future marker
  He will take a plane to Chicago next week. He won't take a bus.

- A polite request
  Will you drive me to the airport?

- An offer
  I will drive you to the hospital for your monthly appointments.

Use *might* (*might not*) to signify:

- Present or future possibility
  He might drive to school, or he might not. He might walk.

Expanding on the Lesson

Bring bus or train schedules to class. Discuss getting around the city using **mass transit**.

Make a carpool chart in class. Have students sign up.

Discuss these additional questions:

- Was life easier or more difficult before the **invention** of mass transit?

- How would teleportation change the world? Give examples.

- What are some transportation problems in your city?

Lesson 5 — Pets

Vocabulary New Words

		Let's Talk Words	
animal	most	abuse	take care of
bullfight	neglect	animal rights group	treat
chicken fight	part of	buy	_____
definition	people	dislike	_____
dictionary	pet	feel	_____
dog race	shelter	find	_____
ever	such as	grow up	_____
human	unusual	guess	_____

Irregular Verb Forms

Base Form	Past	Past Participle
buy	bought	bought
feel	felt	felt
find	found	found
grow	grew	grown

Grammar Focus

Present perfect with *ever*

Use *ever*:

- In questions
  Have you ever had a pet?
  Have you ever gone to a horse race?

- When the exact time the action occurred in the past is not relevant
  Have you ever been to Las Vegas?
  Have you ever seen Gone with the Wind?

Other uses of present perfect: (Lesson 1)

- Past action that continues to the present
  I've had my dog for two years.

- Recently completed action
  Sally has just bought a cute little dog.

- Past experience or action with current relevance
  Bill's dogs haven't felt very well lately.

Expanding on the Lesson

Have students name popular breeds of these pet animals:

- dogs
- cats
- birds
- horses
- fishes
- snakes

Ask students these questions:

- What jobs do animals do for humans? What do you think about animal **labor**?
- How do you feel about using animals for **experiments**? in **medical research**? in **cosmetic** research?
- How do you feel about **fur coats**?
- What toys for animals have you seen in the stores?
- How do you feel about people buying toys for animals?

Job Interviews

Vocabulary New Words

job skill	prepare	application	last
interview	ask	best way	network
employer	hire	duty	possible
characteristic	fire	experience	reference
company	get	expression	reliable
question	look for	guide	salary
employment	file	hiring practices	state
alphabetically	answer	important	supervisor

Let's Talk Words

Irregular Verb Forms

Base Form	Past	Past Participle
get	got	gotten

Grammar Focus

Gerund

A gerund is the *-ing* form of the verb used as a noun.
Studying hard is necessary. Knowing how to operate a computer is important.

Use gerunds as nouns:

- In subject position
  Filing is an important job skill. Working is rewarding.

- In object position
  He's happy about getting the raise.

- In predicate position
  Bill avoids firing employees whenever he can.

Expanding on the Lesson

Have students prepare for a job search by

- writing **resumes**.
- writing **cover letters**.
- **looking through want ads** in newspapers.
- reading **trade magazines** in their field.

Have students go to a local department store, restaurant, or market, and ask for a job application. Fill out the applications in class the next day.

Find out more about students' job knowledge and experience. Ask them these questions:

- What job do you have now?

- What do you like about your job? What do you dislike about it? Why?

- Where are some new or unusual places you can look to find job opportunities?

- How can you start your own company? How can you get the money you might need?

Lesson 7   The Best of Everything

Vocabulary New Words

active	nice
attractive	noisiest
best	quietest
everything	sell
explain	shortest
friendliest	talkative
happiest	tallest
history (of)	variety (of)

Let's Talk Words

ago	newspaper
choice	reviewer
choose	saddest
contest	shop
embarrass	winner
frustrate	worst
local	_____
magazine	_____

Irregular Verb Forms

Base Form	Past	Past Participle
choose	chose	chosen
sell	sold	sold

Grammar Focus

Adjective superlatives

Use adjectives to describe nouns.

Use the superlative form of the adjective to denote that which surpasses all others. Three or more persons or things require the superlative.

- Use the definite article *the* as part of the superlative.
  We have the nicest students in our school.
  Sam is the happiest man I know.
  Jill is the most talkative person in her family.

Rules for using the superlative:

- Add *-est* to a one-syllable adjective.
  Jose is the tallest student in the class.

- Add *-st* to a one syllable adjective that ends in *e*.
  Maria is my nicest cousin.

- Change *y* to *i* and add *-est* to a two-syllable adjective ending in *y*.
  What was the happiest moment in your life?

- Use *most* in front of a two-syllable adjective not ending in *y*, or an adjective with more than two syllables.
  What was the most interesting movie you have ever seen?

- Some common *irregular* adjective superlatives:
  good = *the best*   *Sam's Restaurant has the best chicken.*
  bad = *the worst*   *Gina is the worst cook.*
  far = *the farthest*   *Who lives the farthest from the school?*

Expanding on the Lesson

Ask the class these questions.

In your native country what is the best . . .

- place to **raise a child**?
- town for **entertainment**?
- pet to have?

- hotel for a vacation?
- way to find a job?
- way to **spend free time**?

Have students write ten things they like best. Collect the papers. Read the individual lists to the class. Have students guess who wrote each list.

Family

Vocabulary New Words

aunt	male
brother	mother
children	nephew
daughter	niece
family	parent
family tree	relative
father	sibling
female	sister
grandfather	son
grandmother	spouse
grandparent	uncle
husband	wife

Let's Talk Words

a lot	perfect
approach	related to
argue	teach
avoid	together
childhood	_____
cousin	_____
describe	_____
generous	_____
get along with	_____
in-law	_____
member	_____
occupation	_____

Irregular Verb Forms

Base Form	Past	Past Participle
teach	taught	taught

Grammar Focus

Review of adjectives (General review)

Use adjectives to describe nouns.
He is an honest man. They are nice people.

- Compare two or more persons or things with adjective comparatives.
  Joel is more honest than Hal. Sally's dog is nicer than Jane's dog.

- Denote that which surpasses all others with the superlative form.
  Lilia is the most honest person in the school. Jorge is the nicest man in town.

Review of present/past/present perfect (Lesson 1)

Present

- Habitual actions in the present *I write to my family every week.*
- Uses with stative verbs, especially be *He is my uncle.*
- Present perceptions and emotions *She loves her brother.*

Past

- Action that began and was completed at a point of time in the past
  They saw their father last Sunday. She went shopping with her mother yesterday.

Present perfect

- Past action that continues to the present. *I've been married for six years.*
- Recently completed action. *He's just graduated from high school.*
- Past experience or action with current relevance. *I've missed him since he left.*

Expanding on the Lesson

Have students bring to class a photo album or a home video of their wedding or a family party. Have them explain to the class their relation to the people in the pictures or video.

Refer to **Exercise B. Think** on page 32. What other adjectives can students use to describe their family members? Have students work in pairs and make a list of adjectives that correspond to each of their family members. Write a master list of all adjectives. Discuss.

Ask students these additional questions:
- What is important about being part of a family?
- What other **lifestyles** do people you know have?
- How do you see the **role of family** twenty years from now?

Gender Roles

Vocabulary New Words

accomplishment
change
chore
congratulate
date

gender
get paid (for)
go (out)
home
household
leadership
look up to
make
marriage

men
nowadays
outside
past
respect
role
society
traditionally
typically

usually
who
whom
women
work

Let's Talk Words

expect
house
laundry
modern
put (away)
put (out)
take (out)
  trash

traditional
typical
women's rights
  movement

_____
_____
_____
_____

Grammar Focus

Phrasal verbs

A phrasal verb consists of a verb and one or more particles (preposition or adverb).
Tom took out Beth last Friday.

- Phrasal verbs can be separable (a noun can follow or come between the verb and the particle).
  Ken put his clothes away.

- Some phrasal verbs are inseparable.
  His sister does not get along with him.

- Phrasal verbs can keep their literal meaning.
  The boys took out the trash.

- Phrasal verbs can have a figurative meaning.
  Susie looks up to her grandmother for help.

Expanding on the Lesson

Have students write down all the roles they take on in their life. Then have them circle the roles that are most important to them. Survey the class. Find out which roles students value most.

Ask students if they would prefer a man, a woman, or neither to:

- watch their **newborn** babies
- discuss their **marital** problems
- be president of their country
- **pick up** their garbage

- put new **roofs** on their houses
- give them complete **physicals**
- work in the fire department
- serve in their country's military

Think of other roles men and women **have taken on** and discuss them in class. Ask the students these questions:

- What do you want to change **with regard to** men's and women's roles? Why?

- In the United States, some women **complain** about a "**glass ceiling**" in the workplace. Is there a glass ceiling for working women in your country?

- What is **androgyny**? How would you feel about an **androgenous society**?

Holidays

Vocabulary New Words

holiday
interesting
pay
place
reason
special
young

celebrate
cover
dictate

Let's Talk Words

Dr. Martin Luther
  King, Jr. Day
Father's Day
Halloween
Independence Day
lonely
Memorial Day
Mother's Day

New Year's Day
tell
Thanksgiving
Valentine's Day
Veteran's Day
Washington's Birthday
work

Irregular Verb Forms

Base Form	Past	Past Participle
pay	paid	paid
tell	told	told

Grammar Focus

Review of superlatives (Lesson 7)

Use the superlative form of the adjective to denote that which surpasses all others. Three or more persons or things require the superlative.

- Use the definite article *the* as part of the superlative.

- Add *-est* to a one-syllable adjective. *Bill is the quietest student in the class.*

- Add *-st* to a one-syllable adjective that ends in *e*. *Mother's Day is the nicest holiday.*

- Change *y* to *i* and add *-est* to a two-syllable adjective ending in *y*. *New Year's Day is the happiest holiday of the year.*

- Use *most* in front of a two-syllable adjective not ending in *y*, or an adjective with more than two-syllables. *What is the most important holiday in your country?*

- Some common irregular adjective superlatives are:
  good = *the best*   *Which holiday do you like the best?*
  bad = *the worst*   *Valentine's Day is the worst holiday for lonely people.*

More present/past/present perfect (Lessons 1, 2, and 8)

Present

We celebrate Mother's day every year. Halloween is the scariest holiday.
We like Thanksgiving Day. Our family celebrates many holidays together.

Past

Jack worked last New Year's Day. Cynthia had a wonderful Valentine's Day.

Present perfect

I've seen my family every holiday. We've just eaten a wonderful Thanksgiving dinner.
Holidays have given me special childhood memories.

Expanding on the Lesson

Hold an *International Day* celebration. Have students wear holiday clothing from their native countries. Ask them to bring in some holiday food and music. Discuss the holidays in class. Eat holiday foods and dance to holiday music.

Ask the class these questions:
- What holiday is **coming up**? How and why do people celebrate it?
- What are some important **religious** holidays that you celebrate?
- How and why do you celebrate them?

Lesson 11   Superstitions

Vocabulary   New Words

	catch	salt
	four-leaf clover	spill
	good luck	superstition
	horseshoe	sweep
bad luck	ladder	true
believe	lucky	umbrella
black cat	mirror	under
bouquet	open	walk
break	rabbit's foot	wedding

Let's Talk Words

get married   _____
happen   _____
invent   _____
say   _____
secret   _____
unlucky   _____
unmarried   _____
_____   _____
_____   _____

Irregular Verb Forms

Base Form	Past	Past Participle
break	broke	broken
catch	caught	caught
spill	spilt	spilt
sweep	swept	swept

Grammar Focus

Present real conditional

Use the present real conditional in the *if clause* to show:

- Future plans or possibilities
  If I catch the wedding bouquet, I'll get married soon.
  You'll have bad luck if a black cat crosses your path.

- A weaker conclusion with *might*
  If he walks under a ladder, he might have bad luck.

Say and *tell*

Say and *tell* have similar meanings. They can be used in

- Direct speech with quotations to repeat someone's exact words.
- Reported speech (Lesson 14) to repeat the ideas of a spoken message.

The choice between *say* and *tell* is determined by the use of an indirect object.

- When you use *tell*, an indirect object is usually needed to identify the listener.
  Kim always tells her granddaughter stories about superstitions.

- When you use *say*, an indirect object is optional. The direct object usually
  follows *say*.
  Lisa always says nice things (to Bill). Rob said, "Be careful today. It's Friday the 13th!"

Expanding on the Lesson

Here are other superstitions. Ask students what might happen if:

- their left eye **itches**.   • their left hand itches.   • they eat from a **pot**.
- their right eye itches.   • their right hand itches.   • they **step on** a **crack**.

Horoscopes are modern superstitions. Copy the horoscope section of a newspaper.
Have students form into groups according to their **astrological sign**. Encourage
them to discuss their own **personality traits**. How are they **alike**? Tell them to
read their horoscopes. Do they believe their horoscopes will **come true**?

Sleep

Vocabulary   New Words

always
blanket
daily
day off
dream

get (up)
go (to bed)
good night
hour
lullaby
never
nightmare
often
position
rarely

schedule
sleep
sleeping aid
sleepwalk
snore
sometimes
tired
tuck in

Let's Talk Words

alarm clock
allow
enough
noise
oversleep
ring
scream
sing
sound

wake up
_____
_____
_____
_____
_____
_____
_____
_____

Irregular Verb Forms

Base Form	Past	Past Participle
dream	dreamt	dreamt
oversleep	overslept	overslept
ring	rang	rung
sing	sang	sung
sleep	slept	slept
wake	woke	woken

Grammar Focus

Adverb of frequency

Use an adverb of frequency to describe how often an event or series of events occurs. Note that the adverb precedes the verb.

- These are approximate percentages:

always	=	100%	*I always sleep with a blanket.*
usually	=	80% - 90%	*My wife usually snores.*
often	=	70% - 80%	*They often go to bed late.*
sometimes	=	40% - 60%	*Sometimes we see people sleeping in the park.*
rarely	=	5% - 10%	*I rarely sleep on the beach.*
never	=	0%	*We never use sleeping aids.*

Review of present (Lessons 1, 2, 8, and 11)

- Habitual actions in the present
I always get up early. They never sleep late.

- Uses with stative verbs, especially *be*
She is a light sleeper.

- Present perceptions and emotions
She likes to sleep eight hours a day.

Expanding on the Lesson

Ask students to think about the following:

- What words are associated with sleep? (*bed, pillow, tired . . .*) Have students work in groups. How many words can students name? Have each group write a list. See which group forms the longest list.

Ask the students these questions.

- Do you **fall asleep** with the music on? with the TV on? with a book in your hand? How often?

- What do you do when you want to sleep but you have to stay awake? How do you **keep from** falling asleep?

Stealing

Vocabulary New Words

age	less
chronically	person
common	punishment
fewer	someone
frequently	steal
	thief

Let's Talk Words

criminal	victim
future	violent
hide	_____
judge	_____
rob	_____
robbery	_____

Irregular Verb Forms

Base Form	Past	Past Participle
hide	hid	hidden
steal	stole	stolen

Grammar Focus

Adjective comparatives: *less* versus *fewer*

Less and *fewer* are the negative (opposite) of *more*.

- *Fewer . . . than* is used before count nouns when making a comparison.
  Bill's store has fewer TVs than Jack's store.

  The jewelry store had fewer diamonds in its front window after the robbery.
  (That is, fewer diamonds than it had before the robbery).

- *Less . . . than* is used before non-count nouns when making a comparison.
  Linda has less money saved than her sister does.
  The bank had less money in the vault after the robbery.

Expanding on the Lesson

Ask the local police department to send an officer to your classroom to discuss crime **prevention**. Later have students discuss in class the ideas presented. Ask the students how each of them could help their communities reduce crime.

Let your students be the judge. What punishments (if any) would they give people for stealing . . .

- food to feed their children?
- sports cars to go on **joy rides**?
- anything to sell to pay their rent?

- medicines from **pharmacies** for sick friends?
- money to buy alcohol?
- jewelry to give as a gift?

More questions for students to think about and discuss:

- What is a **pickpocket**? How can you protect yourself from pickpockets?

- What is **cleptomania**? Do you believe that cleptomania is a disease, or do you think it is an excuse for stealing?

- What do you think about governments that **cut off** people's hands for stealing?

- Do you know of any other **cruel** punishments given to people? Does your country's government have limits to the kind of punishment people can receive for stealing?

- If you know a store cashier hasn't charged you enough for a product, do you tell the clerk? If you don't, are you stealing from the store? What if the clerk gives you too much change? What is the **ethical** thing to do in these situations?

Lesson 14

Gossip

Vocabulary New Words

article	loud
continue	news
false	recently
fill	spread
gossip	whisper
hear	wrong

Let's Talk Words

right _____

_____ _____

_____ _____

_____ _____

_____ _____

Irregular Verb Forms

Base Form	Past	Past Participle
hear	heard	heard
spread	spread	spread

Grammar Focus

Reported speech

Use direct speech with quotations when repeating someone's exact words.
Becky said, "I love to listen to gossip."

Use reported speech when repeating the ideas of a spoken message
(not necessarily word for word).

Becky said she loved to listen to gossip.

Direct speech can be changed to reported speech.

- If the direct speech is in the present, reported speech changes tense to the past.
  Susie said, "Billy is so handsome." Susie said Billy was so handsome.

- If the direct speech is in the past, present perfect, or past perfect, reported speech changes tense to the past perfect.
  John said, "Ben got married." John said Ben had gotten married.
  Kay said, "I haven't seen Marge in a long time." Kay said she hadn't seen Marge in a long time.

- If the direct speech contains a modal, reported speech uses a past modal.
  Tina said, "Kim can write well." Tina said Kim could write well.

Expanding on the Lesson

Have students form into groups. Have them imagine they write for a world-famous talk show. Tell them to brainstorm ideas for their show. Then have them write a list of as many discussion topics for their show as they can. What topics do they suggest? Which ones are **taboo**?

More questions on gossip:

- How can false **rumors** or gossip **ruin** someone's career or marriage?

- Can gossip ever be positive? Have your class think of ways gossip might help people in certain situations. Discuss as a class.

- What **talk radio** and TV programs are popular in your area?

- What topics do they talk about?

- What is **slander**? How is it different from gossip?

Lesson 15 Ghosts and the Supernatural

Vocabulary New Words

careful	investigate	séance
create	know	search
creature	leave (behind)	should
Earth	look (like)	space ship
event	mysterious	strange
exist	phenomena	supernatural
free	phenomenon	UFO
ghost	planet	understand
imagine	present	witness

Let's Talk Words

eye witness
hold (a séance)
legal
make contact (with)
spend
take (place)
_____
_____
_____

Irregular Verb Forms

Base Form	Past	Past Participle
hold	held	held
know	knew	knew
leave	left	left
spend	spent	spent
understand	understood	understood

Grammar Focus

Modal *should* (*shouldn't*)

Should conveys the opinion of the speaker (it is a weaker form of *ought to*).
Fred saw a ghost? I think he should take a day off from work and relax.

Use *should* to:

- Give a suggestion
  You should read the new literature about ghosts. It is fascinating.

- Ask for advice
  I saw a UFO in my backyard. Should I call the police?

Expanding on the Lesson

Put all the chairs into a circle. Turn on a flashlight or light a small candle. Close the lights and the blinds. Have the students think back to their childhood. Have them take turns telling scary ghost stories to the class. See who can tell the scariest story.

Many religious books include stories about supernatural events. Ask students to give examples of supernatural stories or events described or **predicted** in their religious books.

Now ask these additional questions:

- Why do you think people **hesitate** to report that they have seen a ghost?

- Do you think the police believe people who report UFOs or ghosts?

- What does **clairvoyant** mean?

- What is **telekinesis**? Do you know anyone who has **telekinetic** powers?

- Halloween is a **spooky** holiday. Some people celebrate it by **dressing up** in costumes and attending a Halloween party. Children usually wear **scary costumes**, such as a ghost or **goblin**, and **knock** on neighbors' doors and ask for candy. What other spooky holidays do people celebrate? How do they celebrate them?

Vocabulary New Words

appropriate	lazy		
boyfriend	love		
break up	relationship		
consider	sloppy		
difficult	teenager		
girlfriend	would		
impolite			

Let's Talk Words

approve	generation
bring home	judge
care about	potential
constant	race
culture	religion
decide	_____
disapprove	_____

Irregular Verb Forms

Base Form	Past	Past Participle
bring	brought	brought

Grammar Focus

Present unreal conditional

A *conditional* sentence states a relationship between cause and effect. The present unreal conditional tense shows a hypothetical (unlikely to occur) or counterfactual (impossible) idea, action, or event.

- Use the past form of the verb in the *if clause* (the cause) to express a present imaginary action.
  If Val had more time, she would date more often.
  If Claire were younger, she would have another child.
  If you disapproved of a family member's relationship, would you tell that person?

- Use *would* or *could* (followed by the base form of the verb) in the *effect* (result) *clause.*
  If they wanted to get married, they would marry each other.
  He would never marry a woman if his family disapproved of her.

Expanding on the Lesson

Ask the class what characteristics they heard in the students' answers to questions one and two in their book (page 62). List the characteristics on the chalkboard. Now have the class number the characteristics in order of importance. Do the students agree with each other? If not, do their opinions **diverge** according to country, gender, or something else?

Ask volunteers to tell the class about their first boyfriend or girlfriend. How did they meet? How did their parents react? What happened to the relationship?

Has anyone in class ever gone out on a **blind date**? Who set up the date? Did the student have a nice time?

In some countries marriages are arranged. Ask the students to think about this while answering these questions:

- Is love necessary for marriage? Why or why not?
- Can people learn to love someone, or is there **chemistry** between people that can't be invented? Explain.
- What does the expression **love is blind** mean?
- What is **love at first sight**? Do you believe it exists?
- What does **falling in love** mean?
- What is love?

Stress

Vocabulary New Words

associate
employee
less than
manage
million

more than
owe
raise
shout
sight
stress

Let's Talk Words

afraid
better
cause
combat
deal with
destroy
handle
mental

negative
nervous
occur
optimist
pessimist
physical
positive
reduce

relax
responsibility
scare
throughout
upset
way
_____
_____

Irregular Verb Forms

Base Form	Past	Past Participle
deal	dealt	dealt

Grammar Focus

Adjective comparatives *less . . . than/more . . . than*

- *Less . . . than* is the opposite of *more . . . than*.
  Raising two children is more stressful than managing a hundred employees.
  Managing a hundred employees is less stressful than raising two children.

- *Less . . . than* is used with non-count nouns, and *less* is separated from *than* by the adjective.
  Discussing a problem is less stressful than arguing about it.
  Walking is less strenuous than lifting weights.

- *Less . . . than* and *more . . . than* can be used to compare other major parts of speech in English.
  These weights weigh more than eight pounds each.
  Julie has less money than Beth.
  Ben weighs more then Matt.

Expanding on the Lesson

Have students choose a problem or stressful situation in their lives and write about it. Tell students **not** to write their names on their papers. Collect the papers and mix them up. Now have students work in pairs. Pass out one paper to each pair. Ask the pairs to discuss the stressful situation and write suggestions for solving or lessening it. Collect the papers; read the problems and solutions to the class. Does the class agree with the ideas given by the paired students?

Work as a class. Have students answer these questions to reflect upon how stress affects them:

- Do you believe that stress can cause a person to become sick? What are some **stress-related** illnesses?

- When you have a lot of stress in your life, how does it affect your work? your relationships with friends and family?

- A wedding can be a positive event that causes stress. What other positive events can cause stress?

Lesson 18 Moving Children Out

Vocabulary New Words

immediate family
issue
move out
remain

Let's Talk Words

across
adult children
advice
down
on your own
over
reaction

regret
_____
_____
_____
_____
_____
_____

Grammar Focus

Review of *say* and *tell* (Lesson 11)

Say and *tell* have similar meanings. They can be used in:

- Direct speech with quotations when repeating someone's exact words.
- Reported speech (Lesson 14) when repeating the ideas of the spoken message.

The differences between *say* and *tell* are the position and use of the indirect object.

- When using *tell,* the indirect object is used to identify the listener. The object (direct or indirect) appears immediately following *tell.*
  His father told him about the time when he moved out of his parents' house.
  Their grandmother told them beautiful stories.

- When using *say,* an indirect object is optional. When it is used, it can never immediately follow *say.*
  Lilia said, "Please move out" to her thirty-eight-year-old son.
  Beth said she wanted her son to move out when he turned twenty-nine.

Expanding on the Lesson

What are the **benefits** of living at home with parents? What are the **disadvantages**? Divide the class in half. Ask half of the class to give **advantages** to living at home as an adult child. Ask the other half to respond with disadvantages. List the answers on the chalkboard. Which list is longest? Which has the most **valid** reasons?

Refer to **Exercise B. Think** on page 72. Start a list on the chalkboard of items to give an adult child when he or she moves out. Ask volunteers to add to the list. Then discuss with the class which items are the most necessary.

Ask students these questions:

- Why do you think adult children move out of their parents' home even when their parents want them to stay?

- How can parents prepare children for moving out when they become adults?

- Where are some places young adults might live after they move out of their parents' home (college **dormitory**, apartment with **roommates**, religious house, **hostel** . . .).

- Sometimes young adults move out of their parents' home to **cohabitate** with someone they love. How do you feel about this?

- Why do some young children run away from home? What local services are available to help **runaway** children?

Lesson 19

Growing Old

Vocabulary New Words

accomplish
achieve
grow (old)
make a
 difference
old
senior citizèn
take turns

Let's Talk Words

advantage
affect
ail
cane
care
convalescent
 hospital
depict
distinguished
elderly
fear

golden years
help
how old
leader
lifestyle
mandatory
media
negative light
nursing home
pass away
plan

positive light
recognized
reflect
refuse
retirement
wheel chair

_____
_____
_____
_____
_____

Grammar Focus

Pronunciation of past regular verbs

The pronunciation of the final -ed in the past form of regular verbs is based upon the letter *sound* immediately preceding the -ed.

- -ed is pronounced [t] when it follows a voiceless consonant. (excluding the consonant "t").
  The senior citizens group worked *hard last week.*
  The elderly man next door baked *delicious cookies for us.*

- -ed is pronounced [d] when it follows a vowel sound or voiced consonant (excluding "d").
  We learned *a lot from our grandparents.*
  They studied *hard to pass the test.*
  They listened *to their grandfather play the violin.*

- -ed is pronounced [id] when it follows the consonants *t* or *d.*
  When we were younger, we visited *our grandparents every month.*
  Joel's grandmother planted *flowers last year.*
  Sam needed *to spend less in order to save for his retirement.*

Expanding on the Lesson

Have students take out the pictures they drew for **Exercise C** on page 76. How does the class view aging?

Continue the discussion on aging by asking the students the following questions:

- If you could **retain** the body of a twenty-five-year-old or have the **mind** of a healthy ninety-year-old for the **rest of your life**, which would you choose?

- What do you think is the most difficult thing about being old?

- Do you think that old people are lonelier than young people? Why or why not?

- Do you think that old people should be **kept alive** on **respirators** and other **artificial** machines? How do you feel about **euthanasia**?

- What do you think happens to people after they die?

Pollution and Recycling

Vocabulary New Words

	glass
	noise pollution
	paper
	plastic
aluminum	pollute
bottle	pollution
can	problem
garbage	recycle

smog
store
styrofoam
waste

Let's Talk Words

active	environmental
concern	group
conserve	force
contribute	frequent
convince	gasoline
depend on	improve
director	recycling center
earth	resources
eliminate	safe
	volunteer

Grammar Focus

Passive voice

Use the passive voice when the result of the action, not the doer, is emphasized.

- Place the direct object in subject position.
  People recycle cans. Cans are recycled by people.

- The subject, now in object position, is frequently deleted.
  Cans are recycled by people. Cans are recycled.

- Use the verb *be* (to show the tense) and the past participle. Students often think of passive voice in the past. Remind them that the passive voice, like the active voice, takes varying tenses.
  Glass bottles and aluminum cans are always recycled (by Denise).
  The bottles and cans were recycled (by Denise).
  The bottles and cans have been recycled (by Denise).

Expanding on the Lesson

Start recycling in your school. Get a few boxes and label them: aluminum cans, glass bottles, newspapers, and other **recyclables**. Have a volunteer student take the recyclables to a center once a month. If your state pays a refund on bottles, save the money. Ask students what they would like to do with the money. (**Donate** it to an environmental group, give it to a local **charity** . . .)

Ask students these questions:

- How can people in your country conserve more of your country's resources? What about the people in the United States?

- What are some other important environmental issues? (Ask students to write their ideas on the chalkboard.)

- How can we keep from polluting our air? Are there cleaner burning fuels available? What do you think about electric or **solar** cars?

- **Offshore** oil **drilling** and oil spills cause pollution in our oceans. What can be done about this problem?

- In a world with **finite** resources, recycling is important. What things not being recycled now might need to be recycled in the future?

Lesson 21 The Homeless and Welfare

Vocabulary New Words

anyone
find out
homeless
represent
services
social worker
someone
welfare

Let's Talk Words

aid
assist
business
change (money)
cross out
depressed
food stamps
give reasons
hunger
in order for
individual
job counselor

jobless
low cost
 housing
needs
offer
poverty
private
profession
program
provide
public assistance
receive

specific
success
successful
suggest
support
system
the best way
unemployed
unhealthy
utility rates
_____
_____

Irregular Verb Forms

Base Form	Past	Past Participle
give	gave	given

Grammar Focus

Some and any

Some and *any* describe the quantity of a noun. Alone they function as pronouns.

Use *any*:

- In negative sentences
  I'm sorry, I don't have any change.

- In negative answers
  Do you have any job openings? No, I'm sorry we don't have any.

Use *some*:

- In positive sentences
  Pat gave some money to the homeless charity drive.

- In positive answers
  Could you give me some change? Sure, here's some.

Expanding on the Lesson

Have students form into groups. Let them discuss the **criteria** needed for a person to be **eligible** for welfare benefits. Then have them write a welfare **recipient** law.

How can society help homeless people who also are dealing with . . .

- **drug addiction**?
- recurring physical illnesses?
- **alcohol abuse** problems?

- extreme **handicaps**?
- **mental illness**?
- social **behavioral** problems?

Discuss these additional questions:

- Are social problems the **responsibility of society**, the individual, or the individual's family, or is the government responsible for healing these problems?

- What are some important social problems in your country?

- Describe a perfect world. Then write a paragraph **illustrating** your ideas.

Disasters

Vocabulary New Words

bomb
category
disaster
drought
earthquake

fire
flood
food
  poisoning
insect
  infestation
natural
  disaster
oil spill
plague

storm
tornado
volcano
war

Let's Talk Words

blow
damages
dinosaur
disaster proof
effect
erupt
extinct
flock
food supply
futuristic
guarantee

homeowner
human race
insurance
policy
insure
lack of
major
natural
resource
pattern
population

predict
roam
salesperson
scientist
survival
unseasonable
use up
useful
weather
_____
_____

Irregular Verb Forms

Base Form	Past	Past Participle
blow	blew	blown

Grammar Focus

Future perfect

Use the *future perfect* tense for an action or state that is expected to
happen or be completed in the future prior to another future time or event.
We will have finished all the construction work on the shelter by 6:00 p.m. tonight.

Use *will*, the auxiliary *have*, and the past participle to form the future perfect.
*They will have bought sand bags for their house before the end of summer and
the start of the rainy season.*

Expanding on the Lesson

Refer to the *Usage* exercise on page 85 of the student text. Copy this chart on the
chalkboard. Ask volunteers to add other items to the appropriate columns (*Natural
disasters* or *Other disasters*). As each list grows, ask the students if they can find a main
difference between the disasters in each column. Ask, "If the other disasters aren't
natural, what are they?" Try to elicit names for the disasters in this category.
Encourage students to say: *unnatural, created,* **accidental**, or **man-made**.

What **supplies** can prevent or **minimize** damages before, during, or after disasters?
Have students form into groups and make a list of **emergency** supplies. Discuss
which items could be needed for each disaster (some ideas: **sand bags**, flashlights,
first aid kits). See which group will be the most prepared for future disasters.

Organize an emergency plan to **cope** with a possible disaster. Work in small groups to
make maps for **escape routes** from your classroom to outside the school. Decide
who will be in charge. Who will check for **injured** people? Who will run for help?

What other verbs are used to show the action of disasters? For example, **shake**
(shook, shaken) is used to show the action of earthquakes.

Ask students these additional questions:

• What disaster do you fear most? Why?

• Why do you think the news media focuses on disasters rather than on positive news?

• Why do you think natural disasters exist?

Smoking

Vocabulary New Words

ban
cigarette
correct
dash
debate
farmer
gallows

hang
hangman
idea
incorrect
industry
non-smoker
smoke
smoker
spell
tobacco

Let's Talk Words

bad habit
bother
break a habit
cancer
chew
could
determine
illegal
instead
permit
quit

second-hand smoke
since
surgeon general
tempt
try

_____
_____
_____
_____
_____
_____

Irregular Verb Forms

Base Form	Past	Past Participle
hang	hanged or hung	hung
quit	quit	quit

Grammar Focus

Could as probability

Could can be used to:

- Make a general request
  Could you smoke outside, please.

- Ask permission
  Could I come to your Smokers Anonymous group?

- Show probability of an action occurring
  Could he have gotten cancer from smoking?

- Convey present meaning
  Could you reach the cigarettes on the table?

Could is also used to express ability in the past
He could run faster two years ago. (He didn't smoke then.)

Review of *should* (Lesson 15)

Should can be used to:

- Convey an opinion
  Everyone who smokes should go to a clinic to break the habit.

- Give a suggestion or ask for advice
  You should stop smoking and improve your health. Should I give up desserts?

Expanding on the Lesson

Have students find **advertisements** for cigarettes in magazines , newspapers, and on billboards. Tell them to bring in copies of the **ads**. (For **billboards** have the students write down what the ad says and remember the picture.) Hang the ads around the classroom. Discuss how the ads make cigarettes **appealing**. Ask students why they think these ads help sell cigarettes.

Now have students work in small groups. Ask each group to create an ad that shows the negative effects of cigarette smoking. Have groups present their ads to the class.

Ask the students:

- Do you think smoking is as harmful as most doctors **claim**? If so, why is it legal?

Gambling

Vocabulary New Words   *Let's Talk* Words

beat (the odds)
brainstorm
enroll
friendship
gamble
game
job placement

life
location
mean (signify)
pay off
purchase
residence
show
take a chance
win

addiction
alcohol
attend
beg
bet
bingo
cheat
crime
cycle
excitement
famous

force
form
fulfill (dreams)
Gambler's
Anonymous
hope
horse races
lie
lottery
make a bet
overeat

overwork
poker
recovery
revenue
self-help
group
site
slot machine
town
_____
_____

Irregular Verb Forms

Base Form	Past	Past Participle
beat	beat	beaten
bet	bet	bet
mean	meant	meant
win	won	won

Grammar Focus

Review of present perfect with *ever* (Lesson 5)

Use *ever*:

- In questions
  Have you ever gambled and won a lot of money?
  Have you ever bet money on a horse race?

- When the exact time the action occurred in the past is not relevant
  Have you ever gone to a famous gaming town?

Review of other present perfect uses (Lessons 1 and 10)

- Past action that continues to the present
  I've lived here for three years.

- Recently completed action
  Alice has just won a large jackpot prize.

- Past experience or action with current relevance
  Kim has already learned how to play Black Jack.

Expanding on the Lesson

Refer to **Let's Start** on page 93. Recreate the chart on the chalkboard. Ask students to volunteer the information on their charts. Write all the decisions students have taken a chance on. Discuss why **taking a risk** or taking a gamble is important in **developing a full life**.

Have students name some forms of saving money that **involve** risk. Do they think these types of **investing** are the same as or are similar to gambling?

Ask these additional questions:

- Do you think more or fewer people will gamble in the future? Why?

- What new forms of gambling do you **envision** for the future? (Think about all the new **technology** available, and imagine gambling on the **internet**.)

- What were some of the most difficult decisions (gambles) you had to make in your life?

Lesson 25   War and the Military

Vocabulary New Words

conflict
current
military
neither
nor

Let's Talk Words

both	educate	justify	Red Cross
close	effective	medal	resolve
relationship	engage in	military	reward
defend	enlist	service	risk
devastate	fight	necessary	serve
dilemma	generation	peacetime	soldier
dishonorable	historian	prison	solve
discharge	honorable	punish	United
disobey	discharge	purple heart	Nations
draft	injure	purpose	voluntary
during	involved in	rebuild	wartime

Irregular Verb Forms

Base Form	Past	Past Participle
fight	fought	fought
rebuild	rebuilt	rebuilt

Grammar Focus

Past continuous tense

Use the past continuous tense to:

- Tell a story in the past
  The two countries were fighting over where to draw their borders.

- Show a continuing past action that is interrupted by another past action
  They were watching television when the war started in their city.

- Refer to an action taking place during a period of time in the past
  The United States was fighting Iraq in the Persian Gulf War.

Expanding on the Lesson

Have students think back into their own country's history. What wars do they think could have been avoided? Have students work with people from their native country to rewrite history in order to avoid wars. Then have the students tell the class about their revised history.

Refer to **Exercise B. Think** on page 100. Ask volunteers to write some of their ideas on the chalkboard. As a class, discuss all the ideas.

Other issues to discuss:

- Is world peace possible?

- What countries recognize **dual citizenship**? Does your country?

- Is it possible to be **loyal** to more than one country? What might happen to your loyalty during a war between the countries that you love?

- What is a **civil war**? Have there been any civil wars in your country?

- Are separate countries necessary? What might happen if there were no countries or militaries? Do you think a world government is possible?

Money Management

Vocabulary   New Words

account
already
apply
at least
bill
broke (poor)

budget
charge
cheer up
context
credit card
due
earn
forever
join
luxury

money
management
my treat
of course
paycheck
payment
pay off (bills)
penny
tell me about it

Let's Talk Words

accept
basic
bond (savings)
charity
comfortable
compare
cost
debt
invest

major purchase
manage
  (money)
modify (debts)
nest egg
properly
save
stock
unable
wise

Irregular Verb Forms

Base Form	Past	Past Participle
cost	cost	cost

Grammar Focus

Future *will/be going to*

Use *will* and *going to* to make future predictions.

> *We will owe ninety dollars on our credit card next month.*
> *We are going to owe ninety dollars on our credit card next month.*

- Use *will* to show future willingness.
  Call me anytime. I will help you invest your money wisely.
  Will you accept a job in a different country?
  Are you willing to accept a job in a different country?

- Use *would* to replace *will* if a question is hypothetical.
  Would you accept a job in another country?

- Use *be going to* to show prior plans.
  Why did you save so much money? I'm going to buy a new car.

- Sometimes *will* is seen as more formal than *be going to*.
  I will have the money for you by Friday.

Expanding on the Lesson

Discuss as a class. How much money does it take . . .

- to be comfortable?
- to be **debt free**?
- for a family of four to **live well**?
- to be rich?

Are people ever **satisfied** with their **living standards**, or do they always want more?

More questions on money management:

- What does it mean to **live within your means**?

- What is **bankruptcy**? Why do people file for bankruptcy?

- What does "**barter**" mean? Do you think that life was easier when people bartered for items and didn't use money?

- Do you think paper money will become **obsolete** and people will use only **electronic transactions** to pay for their **purchases**?

Cheating

Vocabulary New Words

anybody
begin
copy
nobody
order
poem

prosper
report
right reason
somebody
view

Let's Talk Words

advertising
business
  transaction
car part
cashier
catch
  cheating
claim
commercial
customer

deceptive
demonstrate
disappoint
exam
get away with
get caught
insurance
mechanic
medical
owner

prestigious
pretend
product
replace
short-change
solution
subject
surgeon
themselves
yourself

Irregular Verb Forms

Base Form	Past	Past Participle
begin	began	begun

Grammar Focus

Indefinite pronouns

An *indefinite pronoun* is used to represent a non-specific person or thing.

***Someone/somebody* is:**

- Used in affirmative sentences
  Someone copied my test.

- Used in a question when the asker assumes the recipient of the question has knowledge of the question's topic, and also assumes that the recipient will answer positively
  Did someone see who copied Sally's test?

***Anyone/anybody* is used in:**

- Negative sentences
  He doesn't know anyone in the class.

- General questions
  Can anyone help me with this question?

- Positive sentences to express generality
  Anybody can pass this class.

No one/nobody is used as the subject of an affirmative sentence that makes a strong statement.

No one cheated on the test.
Nobody failed the class.

Expanding on the Lesson

In what other **aspects of life** do people cheat? Refer to **Exercise B. Think** on page 108. What do people hope to gain by cheating? How can a **loss of credibility** lessen the value of anything **gained** by cheating?

Explain why the following are considered to be cheating:

- **exaggerating** on a resume
- helping a friend with a take-home test
- taking extra time on a work break
- paying someone to write your report

How can cheating be **dangerous** to society?

Lesson 28 Government Spending

Vocabulary New Words

street sign
business loan
wildlife
museum

legal aid
sanitation
grants
disability
  benefits
highway
dental care
medical care
primary

public
require
research
ambulance
unemployment
  benefits
jail
repair
secondary

space
  exploration
mentally ill
government
  spending
benefit
lighting

Let's Talk Words

be in charge
collect
donate
government
  funding
income
inheritance
power
property

tax
wage
_____
_____
_____
_____
_____
_____

Grammar Focus

Review of present unreal conditional (Lesson 16)

The present unreal conditional tense shows hypothetical (unlikely to occur) or counterfactual (impossible) ideas, actions, or events.

- Use the past form of the verb to express a present imaginary action.
  If Steve had extra money, he would donate it to his school.

- Use *if* in the same clause as the past verb.
  If Joe were the budget director, we would save more money.

- Use *would* (followed by the base form of the verb) in the main clause.
  If I were president of my country, I would spend more money on education.
  I would spend more money on education if I were the president of my country.

- Use *Imagine* as another way to show the present unreal conditional.
  Imagine you were in charge of your country's budget. How would you spend its money?

Expanding on the Lesson

A government collects money through taxes. How do other countries **raise** government revenue. Make a double-column chart on the chalkboard. Label one column *Country* and the other *Government revenue*. Have students complete the chart. Here are some ideas:

- police **citations**
- public parking **fees**
- stamps for postage

- government-run lottery
- **toll** roads
- selling **bonds**

- licenses (car, business)
- **recreation** fees
- **non-resident** student fees

Refer to **Exercise C. Write** on page 112 in the student book. Ask volunteers to read their ideas. Discuss as a class.

In the United States, most government programs have budgets. If the budget director doesn't use all the **funds**, they are not available next year. Do you think this is a good **policy**? What budget **restrictions** does your country's government have for its programs?

More questions on government spending:

- Do you think there should be more or fewer government programs?

- Which is more **beneficial** to most people, one large national government or many small local governments?

- What happens to governments that **overspend** their budgets?

- Why do some governments **lend** money to other countries? Do the people of either country usually approve of this?

Lesson 29 Prejudice and Discrimination

Vocabulary New Words

against
aloud
assign
categorize
define
different
discriminate
discrimination
divide
free (of)

label
nationality
prejudice
raise children
separate
size
social status
stereotype

Let's Talk Words

as well as
called (named)
civil right
Constitution
document
entitle to
experience
expose
highest
invite

law
opinion
personal liberties
prevent
protect
World's Rights
   Organization

_____

_____

_____

Grammar Focus

Past perfect

Use the past perfect tense in the main clause:

- To show a past action that occurred before another past action
  By the time I walked in the door and sat down, the personnel director had already stereotyped me.

- With *before* and the simple past in the adverbial clause
  Before the civil rights movement in the United States began, government officials had done little to protect people from prejudice and discrimination.

Expanding on the Lesson

Refer to the **Let's Start** exercise on page 113. What other categories did your class think about? Discuss whether or not those categories are necessary to describe people. How else can people refer to one another? (Other categories: religion, hair color, occupation, **intellect**, hobbies, . . .)

How can prejudice and discrimination be prevented? How can the views of prejudiced people be changed? Refer to **Exercise B. Think** on page 116 in the student book. Ask students to share their ideas. Write a list of ideas on the chalkboard. Discuss them. Then submit the list to your school newspaper.

Ask students to:

- Give examples in history where prejudice and discrimination **destroyed** the lives of many people.

- Name some common characteristics of people who discriminate against others. Ask them why they think **certain** people have these characteristics.

- Show how language can be **sexist** and can discriminate against women (for example: *mankind* meaning *people*). Have students give examples from their languages.

- Think about ways in which people discriminate in their taste for things (foods, drinks, furniture, clothes . . .).

- Write a short paragraph about how they felt when **prejudicial** feelings were personally justified for a particular **incident**. (For example, a woman is walking to her car and sees a man approaching her. She **clutches** her purse.)

Divorce

Vocabulary New Words

acquire	save
asset	(a marriage)
aware	thoughts
divorce	tool
faithful	trust
finish	wish
get divorced	
identity	
react	

Let's Talk Words

agreement	laugh
alimony	lively
be around	marital status
child support	patient
ex-spouse	remain
ex-wife	rich
funny	split
intelligent	wonder
joint custody	_____
kind	_____ _____

Irregular Verb Forms

Base Form	Past	Past Participle
split	split	split

Grammar Focus

Past unreal conditional/*wish*

The past unreal conditional tense is used to express a past imaginary action.

If Lisa had married Joe, she would have had money to travel.

- Use *if* in the same clause as the past perfect tense.
If Sally had known Mike better, she wouldn't have married him.

- Use *would* (followed by the present perfect tense) in the main clause.
Becky would have divorced John if he had been unfaithful to her.

Use *wish*:

- Plus the present unreal conditional
Hal wishes he were married.
Kelly wishes she had a patient husband.

- Plus the past unreal conditional
Steve wishes he had invited his ex-wife to the party.
Their children wish their parents hadn't gotten a divorce.

Expanding on the Lesson

How is divorce viewed by:

- people from different countries?
- people of different religions?
- the older generation?
- the younger generation?

Discuss these issues:

- How does divorce affect a child? Does divorce affect children of different ages differently?

- Should couples stay together "for the children," even if the parents are no longer in love?

- In your country, after parents divorce, does a child have a **legal right** to choose which parent to live with?

- What do you think about **mandatory** marriage counseling for couples who have marital problems?

- How do you feel about **prenuptial agreements**? What about five-year **renewable** marriage **contracts**?

Calling In Sick

Vocabulary New Words

Let's Talk Words

absent
artist
average
call in sick
carpenter
housekeeper
lunch break
painter
personnel

plumber
secretary
sick
various
writer

manager
per
previous
sick day
valid

_____
_____
_____
_____

Grammar Focus

Review of passive voice (Lesson 20)

Use the passive voice to show when the result of an action, not the doer, is emphasized.

- Place the direct object in subject position.
  The company paid Anna for sick days. Anna was paid for sick days by the company.

- The subject, now in object position, is frequently deleted.
  Anna was paid for sick days by the company. Anna was paid for sick days.

- Use the verb *be* (to show the tense) and the past participle. Students often think of passive voice in the past. Remind them that the passive voice, like the active voice, takes varying tenses.
  Employees are usually allowed five sick days a year.
  Employees were allowed five sick days a year at EGO Company last year.
  Employees have been allowed five sick days a year.

- Modals can be used in the passive voice.
  An employee should be allowed sick days with pay.

Expanding on the Lesson

Have students work together in a small group as a personnel team. Tell them to write criteria for receiving **compensation** for workdays missed. Which of these reasons for absence will their company consider valid? Which will not be **compensated** for?

- employee illness
- a day in **court**
- personal problem
- city-wide disaster

- **bereavement**
- sick child
- mental health day
- employee injury

- religious holiday
- transportation problems
- car or property **damage**
- elderly parent care

Encourage students to add their own ideas. Then discuss their answers as a class.

Have students pretend they are in a **management** position. Ask them the following questions:

- How do you feel about parents taking days off to care for their sick children?
- What about people taking days off to care for their sick elderly parents?
- How can employees' **obligations** to their family affect their jobs?
- What would you do if an employee called in sick **excessively** for **legitimate** reasons?
- How do you feel about paying people for unused sick time?

Justice Systems

Vocabulary New Words   *Let's Talk* Words

court case
fair
forget

guilty	arrest	fit (equal)	prisoner
innocent	capital	hindsight	rape
justice	punishment	inmate	right to
justice served	commit	legal system	security
justice system	corporal	look back	send to prison
outcome	punishment	maximum	sentence (court)
phrase	crime of passion	minimum	theft
should have	death row	minor	try in court
verdict	deserve	mistake	_____
	enforce	murder	_____
	fist fight	perspective	_____

Irregular Verb Forms

Base Form	Past	Past Participle
fit	fit	fit
forget	forgot	forgotten
send	sent	sent

Grammar Focus

Modal perfect *should have*

Use *should have* to show regret for past choices.

- Use the positive form to show regret for an action not taken.
  The jury should have found the man guilty of the crime.

- Use the negative form to show regret for an action that was done or taken.
  Larry shouldn't have stolen the car.

Expanding on the Lesson

Have students work in groups to try to decide what causes people to commit crimes. Have the groups list their ideas and share them with the class. If they haven't mentioned the following explanations, suggest them and discuss with the class.

- poverty
- low self-esteem
- no parental guidance
- lack of education
- loss of, or no, religious faith
- lack of job opportunities
- no set of values

Additional questions for class discussion:

- Does the fear of punishment **deter** people from committing crimes? Why or why not?

- Do most punishments fit the crime?

- How have crime and punishment changed over the past fifty years in your country? Give some examples.

- In the United States, **suspects** of crimes are judged by a jury and **sentenced** by a judge. Who judges and sentences criminal suspects in your country?

- What does "justice" mean to you?

Drugs and Medicine

Vocabulary   New Words   *Let's Talk* Words

aspirin
caffeine
classification
cocaine
drug

headache
marijuana
medicine
patient
penicillin
prescription
side effect

ailment
backache
catch selling
catch using
constipation
diarrhea
garlic
generic
ginger root
ginseng

herb
ill
legalize
on the street
over the
  counter
prescribe
rehabilitation
  center
remedy

sore throat
stomachache
stuffy nose
vomit

_____
_____
_____
_____
_____

Grammar Focus

Embedded questions used to show politeness

An embedded question is more polite than a regular question.
Do you know what the side effects of this drug are?

- When a form of *be* is in the embedded question, use regular sentence order.
  What kind of medicine is that? Do you know what kind of medicine that is?

- Where *do* is in the question, it is dropped in the embedded question.
  How much does that medicine cost? Could you tell me how much that medicine costs?

- In an embedded yes-no question, use regular sentence order and add *if* or *whether*.
  Do you know if garlic is an herb? Could you tell me whether I should take aspirin or ginseng for my backache?

Expanding on the Lesson

Encourage students to bring in empty **packaging** from common over-the-counter **medications**. Have them work in groups to read all the **literature information** about the medications. (Each group will work on a different medication.) Have students explain the directions to each other in their own words. When they finish, have them tell the class about the medications. Be sure they can explain:

- **usage**
- general **warnings**
- correct **dosage**
- drug **precautions**
- common side effects
- remedies for **accidental overdose**

Additional questions to talk about:

- How do you feel about **herbal** remedies?

- How can drug-addicted people be helped?

- How can people stop **street vending** of drugs?

- When should over-the-counter medicine *not* be given without a doctor's **recommendation**? (examples: a pregnant woman, a baby, an elderly person who is taking other medications . . .)

- How do you feel about people with **terminal illnesses** using prescribed **experimental** drugs?

Lesson 34 What Would You Do If...

Vocabulary

New Words

conclusion
creative
develop
fluently
logical
paragraph
pound
swell up
translator
weigh

Let's Talk Words

admit
bookkeeper
born
discover
embezzle
fail
final
fond of
grant
human being
kill

magic lamp
notify
overhear
read minds
turn around

_____
_____
_____
_____
_____

Irregular Verb Forms

Base Form	Past	Past Participle
overhear	overheard	overheard
read	read	read

Grammar Focus

Review of present unreal conditional (Lesson 16)

The present unreal conditional tense shows a hypothetical (unlikely to occur) or counterfactual (impossible) idea, action, or event.

- Use the past form of the verb to express a present imaginary action.
  If you were granted three wishes, what would you wish for?
  What would you buy if you won the lottery?

Review of Past unreal conditional (Lesson 30)

The past unreal conditional tense expresses a past imaginary action.

   If we had won the lottery, we would have bought a new car.
   I wouldn't have gotten sick if I hadn't eaten the old food.

More on *wish*

Wish can be used in:

- The present unreal conditional
  I wish I spoke English fluently. I wish I had a job.
- The past unreal conditional
  I wish I had gotten up earlier.

Expanding on the Lesson

Ask students these questions:

- If you had the power to eliminate one illness of your choice, what illness would you eliminate? Why?

- If you could change places with anyone in the world, who would you change places with and why?

- If you hadn't chosen to study English, what would you have done with your time?

Lesson 35

Employment Issues

Vocabulary

New Words

career	section
classified	telecommute
could have	vacation
flexibility	
in house	
job security	
pension plan	
priority	

Let's Talk Words

available	occasional
boss	performance
confront	promote
damage	reputation
directions	_____
following	_____
incentive	_____
might have	_____

Grammar Focus

Perfect modals *could have/might have*

Use *could have* to show:

- Past possibilities
  Helen could have opened the office door this morning.

- That the action referred to was not accomplished
  I could have applied for the management position (but I didn't).

- Past generalities
  John could have gotten any job he wanted.
  They could have hired anyone for that job.

Use *might have* to show:

- Past possibilities with an unknown outcome (Many speakers use *could have* here too.)
  Jack went home early because he might have finished all his work. (I don't know if he finished his work or not.)

- Past possibilities that did not occur
  If she had lifted the heavy machinery, she might have hurt her back. (She didn't hurt her back.)

Teacher's Note: Have students look at the opening sentence of the *Usage* section on page 137 in the student text: "You might have the opportunity to look for a (new) job." Ask students the difference between the words *might have* (modal, verb) and the perfect modal *might have*. Ask students how the meaning would change in the following sentence: You *might have* had the opportunity to look for a new job.

Expanding on the Lesson

Discuss some employment issues or problems students might have or might already have had at a job site. Have them write a situation. Tell them not to write their names on their papers. Collect the papers. Read one employment issue to the class each day and discuss how the situation might have been resolved.

Find out what students feel is most important in making a career choice. Refer to **Let's Start** on page 137. What was the highest priority for career choices? What was the lowest? What other incentives are important when making a career decision?

Ask the students about these employment issues:

- What is **harassment**? What is **sexual harassment**? What should you do if you are harassed at work?

- What does **equal opportunity employment** mean?

- What questions should employers not ask employees during job interviews?

- What questions should employees not ask employers?

Vocabulary

New Words

amusement park	light
attendant	must
cancel	really
estimate	safety
even though	smell
excuse	taste
extremely	terrible
funeral	twice
heavy	
lady	

Let's Talk Words

catch in a lie
difference
make up
request
think back
white lie

_____
_____
_____
_____
_____

Grammar Focus

Modal *must (mustn't)*

Use *must* to show:

- Necessity
  I want to go out to dinner with you, but I really must stay on my diet.

- Obligation
  There was an emergency at the office. I must go in to work immediately.

- Demanded mandatory action
  We won't tolerate any more excuses. You must come to work on time.

Expanding on the Lesson

Here are some **awkward** situations. Should students answer honestly, tell an excuse or lie, or somehow avoid questions about:

- the burnt chicken their spouse cooked?

- their grumpy supervisor?

- their age or their weight?

- their political views?

- their personal finances?

Have students work in pairs. Tell them to make a list of situations where "**white lies**" might be appropriate. Then collect the lists and write students' ideas and white lies on the chalkboard. See if the entire class agrees on the classification of these situations and ideas.

Ask these additional questions:

- What excuses have students in the class used? In what situations did the students feel they had to make up an excuse?

- How can parents teach their children not to lie?

Have the students imagine they are teachers. In pairs, have them write a list of excuses they might hear from students for their absences and tardiness. Then discuss together which excuses have been used in your class.

Lesson 37 Forms of Government

Vocabulary

New Words

capitalism
communism
form of government
information
prime minister
ruler
socialism
world leader

Let's Talk Words

decision
global economy
mention
operate
stand for

_____ _____
_____ _____
_____ _____

Grammar Focus

Questions: present/past/present perfect (Lesson 2)

To form a question:

- With the verb *be*, a modal, or the auxiliary *have*, invert the usual sentence order.
  Is she a world leader? Can capitalism survive in a global economy?
  Have you ever voted?

- When there is no verb *be*, modal, or auxiliary, use the correct tense of the auxiliary *do* before the subject.
  Do people in your country usually vote? Do you have information about the election?

- After the auxiliary *do*, use the base form of the verb (without *to*).
  Did you vote in the last election? What policies does your prime minister stand for?

- When *who* or *what* is the subject, show the verb tense (*do* is not used).
  Who guards the security of your president? Who went to the voting booth (polls) with you?

To the teacher:

Review any grammar focus that seems appropriate for the students. Here are some ideas: present and present perfect, Lesson 1; gerunds, Lesson 6; passive voice, Lesson 20; conditional sentences, Lessons 11, 16, and 30.

Expanding on the Lesson

Have students form into groups. Tell them to make a list of all the great world leaders they know something about. Then copy their lists on the chalkboard. Discuss how these people changed the world.

Ask students these historical questions:

- What do you think about the **collapse** of the Soviet Union? Why?

- How do you feel about the fall of the Berlin wall? Why?

- Do you know of any other recent changes in government in your native country? What are they?

Talk more about how governments **shape the world**. Ask these questions:

- If a global economy were to exist, would independent governments and countries be necessary?

- What does a **"free trade agreement"** mean? How does (or would) this type of agreement affect your country?

Professionalism

Vocabulary   New Words

appearance
character actress
comedian
contract
hair stylist
lawyer

librarian
marketing
  manager
meeting
must have
past life
personality
politician
profession
professionalism
psychic

renewal
review (at work)
TV series
TV show ratings

Let's Talk Words

accountant
background
break down
dishonest
earn a living
employ
ethical
influence
pursue
take
  advantage of

true professional
trustworthy
unethical
unprofessional
unskilled
workforce
_____
_____
_____
_____

Grammar Focus

Perfect modal *must have*

Use *must have* to make a conclusion, inference, or deduction from the evidence.
Jackie is very happy with her job evaluation. She must have gotten a promotion.
Joe is looking through the want ads. He must have lost his job.
Tom took the bus to work last week. He must have had car trouble.
Violet fired her assistant last week. He must have arrived late for work again.

Expanding on the Lesson

Have students work in small groups. Tell them to list as many professions as they can think of and what the people do on those jobs. Write their suggestions on one side of the chalkboard. Then ask all the students what qualifications they think are necessary for each job listed. Write their ideas next to the job. Now ask students which jobs they feel are prestigious. What do all prestigious careers have in common? How do they differ from **blue collar jobs**?

Have students form different small groups. Give them these questions to discuss.

What profession have you always wanted? Do you have the career you want? If so, explain how you achieved your **goal**. If not, what happened in your life to keep you from getting the career you wanted? How could you obtain the employment you desire in the future?

More discussion points:

- The most and least desirable jobs in students' native countries
- Salary effects on evaluation of a profession
- Professions that can change the world
- Illegal jobs or professions. Why are they illegal?
- Unethical or unprofessional behavior

Success

Vocabulary   New Words   *Let's Talk* Words

close friend
decent
integrity
keep
own
possess
possession
powerful
rare
valuable

achievement
anniversary
business contact
generally
goal
in mind
in terms of
keep in touch
network
organize

personal contact
renowned
social life
type of
work hard

_____
_____
_____
_____
_____

Irregular Verb Forms

Base Form (without "to")	Past	Past Participle
keep	kept	kept

Grammar Focus

General review of modals *can/might/must/should*

Use *can (can't)* to show:

- Ability *She can network in this organization.*
- Permission in some questions *Can I keep in touch with you?*
- Request in some questions *Can you organize our network of business contacts?*

Use *might (might not)* to signify:

- Present or future possibility
  He might work hard, or he might not. Let's hire him and find out.

Use *must (mustn't)* to signify:

- Necessity
  I want to work overtime, but my doctor says I must get some rest.
- Obligation
  There was an emergency in my family. I must go home immediately.
- Mandatory action demanded
  You must work hard to be successful at this company.

Use *should* to:

- Convey the opinion of the speaker
  All people who work hard should become successful at what they do.
- Give a suggestion or ask for advice
  You should network to become successful.

To the Teacher:

Review any grammar focus that seems appropriate for the students. Here are some ideas: imperatives, Lesson 3; reported speech, Lesson 14; future and future perfect, Lesson 22.

Expanding on the Lesson

Refer to the **Let's Start** exercise on page 153. Survey the class and find out how each group viewed success. What was their highest priority? What was the lowest? What other types of success did they discuss?

Begin and end the class with a few success stories. Have students get up in front of the class and tell other students what kind of success or accomplishments they have experienced. (Be sure to clap when they finish their stories.) Who would you change places with and why?

Vocabulary   New Words   *Let's Talk* Words

_____   _____   _____   _____
_____   _____   _____   _____
_____   _____   _____   _____
_____   _____   _____   _____
_____   _____   _____   _____
_____   _____   _____   _____
_____   _____   _____   _____

Vocabulary

Look at the vocabulary words students wrote in their boxes.   In your Teacher's Manual, copy the words that appear most frequently in the students' books. Explain these words to the class.

Expanding on the Lesson

Refer back to question 1 on page 158. Have students write some additional questions they want to ask people in the class. Make a master list of questions on the chalkboard. Have students form into groups and ask each other some of the additional questions.

Ask students what careers they hope to have in the future. Discuss where they might find help getting those types of jobs. If some students plan other events in their future (family, more school, travel), have them discuss their future hopes.

Here are some additional topics students might find interesting.

- Marriage and Fidelity
- Clubs and leisure
- Travel
- Illegal Professions
- Government Parties

- Environmental Issues
- Cohabitation
- Roommates
- The Media in Society
- Countries' Symbolism and Gestures

- Raising Children
- Materialism
- Plastic Surgery
- Conformity

Have students write several questions for each topic. Have them work in pairs and ask and answer the questions they wrote.

Ask students to suggest other topics they enjoy talking about. Find out which ones they would add to a conversation book.

Have students describe games people play at parties in their countries. Play some of those games the last day of class.

Get a giant piece of construction paper. Give all students one last chance to say goodbye to you and to each other. Have each student write a few sentences on the paper. Hang it up the last day of class.

Games for Verb Practice

Write Right Fast

Divide your chalkboard in half. Write *Past* on the top of one half and *Past Participle* at the top of the other half. Put a chair next to the center of the chalkboard. Place any small item on the chair (such as a pen, ruler, or paper). Divide the class into two teams. Ask one student from each team to go up to the board. Read the base form of a verb from your verb tense chart. One student writes the past and the other, the past participle. Encourage class participation by having students shout out the answer to their team members. The student who finishes first takes the object off the chair. That student receives a point for his or her team. The team with the most points at the end wins. (Another variation of this game involves giving all students a past verb or past participle on a flash card. All the students with a past verb are part of one team, and all the students with a past participle form the other team. Call out a base form of a verb. The students with the past and past participle of that verb run to the front of the room and put their verb cards on the chalk tray. The fastest student receives the point.)

If You're Wrong, You'll Hang

Play Hangman against the students. (The complete directions for this game can be found on page 89 in the student book.) Write dashes on the chalkboard. Each dash represents one letter in the base form of a verb. As in regular Hangman, students guess letters to complete the word; however, in this version the students don't guess the exact word. Instead they shout out the past and past participle of the verb base form that is growing letter by letter on the chalkboard. Remember, every time a student guesses a wrong letter or word, a body part is drawn on the gallows. Students must guess the correct past and past participle of the verb before they hang, or the teacher gets a point. For example, if there are three blanks and the students guess the letters *ea*, they cannot say *eat*; they must shout out ate and eaten to get a point.

Concentrate on the Verbs

Have all verb base forms on flash cards in one pile, and all the past and past participles mixed up in another. One complete set is needed for each group of students. Have students form into small groups of about ten students. Appoint one student to pass out all the verb base forms equally among his or her group. Another student shuffles the past and past participles and puts them face down on a large table. Students look at their cards. The first student to play turns over a card on the table. (Everyone can see it.) If the student has in his hand the base form card of the past or past participle card showing, the student collects the turned-over card and chooses another card to turn over. If not, the student returns the card face down, and the next student chooses a card. When a student finds the past and past participle cards of the base verb form from the cards he holds, the student eliminates those cards from his or her hand. The first student who is left with no cards wins.

Irregular Verb Tense Chart

Infinitive	Past	Past participle	Infinitive	Past	Past participle
be	was/were	been	leave	left	left
beat	beat	beaten	lose	lost	lost
become	became	become	make	made	made
begin	began	begun	mean	meant	meant
bet	bet	bet	meet	met	met
blow	blew	blown	overhear	overheard	overheard
break	broke	broken	oversleep	overslept	overslept
bring	brought	brought	pay	paid	paid
buy	bought	bought	put	put	put
catch	caught	caught	quit	quit	quit
choose	chose	chosen	read	read	read
cost	cost	cost	rebuild	rebuilt	rebuilt
deal	dealt	dealt	ride	rode	ridden
do	did	done	ring	rang	rung
draw	drew	drawn	say	said	said
dream	dreamed	dreamt	see	saw	seen
drink	drank	drunk	sell	sold	sold
drive	drove	driven	send	sent	sent
eat	ate	eaten	sing	sang	sung
feel	felt	felt	sleep	slept	slept
fight	fought	fought	speak	spoke	spoken
find	found	found	spend	spent	spent
fit	fit	fit	spill	spilled/spilt	spilt
fly	flew	flown	split	split	split
forget	forgot	forgotten	spread	spread	spread
get	got	gotten	stand	stood	stood
give	gave	given	steal	stole	stolen
go	went	gone	sweep	swept	swept
grow	grew	grown	take	took	taken
hang	hung	hung	tell	told	told
have	had	had	teach	taught	taught
hear	heard	heard	think	thought	thought
hide	hid	hidden	understand	understood	understood
hold	held	held	wake	woke	woken
keep	kept	kept	win	won	won
know	know	known			

Tense Forms

Forms of Tenses (aspect) and Modals

Simple Present Tense	Simple Past Tense	Simple Future Tense
Use the base form of the verb. Add an -s to the third person singular form.	Regular verbs end in -ed. For irregular verbs, see the Verb Tense Chart.	Use the present of the verb be, followed by going to and the base form of the verb.
I live in Peru. You live in Japan. He lives in Mexico. She lives in Iran. It lives in Oz. We live in Korea. They live in Russia.	I liked the chicken. You loved the turkey. He liked his sandwich. She finished her salad. It ate the fish. We ate cereal. They drank tea.	I'm going to play soccer. You're going to plant flowers. He's going to watch TV. She's going to buy some clothes. It's going to stay home. We're going to cook. They're going to study.

Present Continuous	Past Continuous	Future Continuous
Use the present of be, followed by the base form of the verb plus -ing.	Use the past of be, followed by the base form of the verb plus -ing.	Use the (modal) future marker will and the base form of be, followed by the base form of the verb plus -ing.
I'm studying English. You're exercising. He's visiting friends. She's working. It's sleeping. We're speaking English. They're sitting in class.	I was singing. You were leaving. He was thinking. She was buying clothes. It was drinking water. We were driving. They were selling food.	I'll be working. You'll be studying. He'll be playing soccer. She'll be cooking dinner. It''ll be eating. We'll be standing in line. They'll be asking questions.

Present Perfect	Past Perfect	Future Perfect
Use the present tense of the auxiliary have, followed by the past participle of the verb.	Use the past tense of the auxiliary have, followed by the past participle of the verb.	Use the (modal) future marker will, followed by the base form of the auxiliary have, followed by the past participle of the verb.
I've studied English. You've eaten. He's visited his friends. She's worked. It's slept. We've sung songs. They've sat in class.	I had sung a lullaby. You had left. He had eaten. She had bought clothes. It had drunk water. We had driven to work. They had sold food.	I'll have worked. You'll have studied. He'll have played soccer. She'll have cooked dinner. It'll have eaten. We'll have bought food. They'll have grown up.

Tense Forms

The base form of the verb follows modals.

Modal *will*	Modal *can*	Modal *should*
I'll study English.	I can sing.	I should work.
You'll eat.	You can dance.	You should study.
He'll visit his friends.	He can drive.	He should cook dinner.
She'll work.	She can buy a car.	She should sleep more.
It'll sleep.	It can fly.	It should eat now.
We'll sing songs.	We can study.	We should buy some food.
They'll sit in class.	They can read.	They should grow up.

Modal *might*	Modal *could*	Modal *must*
I might study English.	I could sing.	I must work.
You might eat.	You could dance.	You must study.
He might visit his friends.	He could drive.	He must cook dinner.
She might work.	She could buy a car.	She must sleep more.
It might sleep.	It could fly.	It must eat now.
We might sing songs.	We could study.	We must buy some food.
They might sit in class.	They could read.	They must grow up.

The auxiliary *have* and the past participle of the verb follow past modals.

Perfect *should have*	Perfect *could have*	Perfect *must have*	Perfect *might have*
I should have studied.	I could have sung.	I must have overslept.	I might have watched TV.
You should have eaten.	You could have danced.	You must have studied.	You might have traveled.
He should have driven.	He could have driven.	He must have cooked dinner.	He might have cooked dinner.
She should have cried.	She could have slept.	She must have worked.	She might have worked.
It should have slept.	It could have flown.	It must have eaten.	It might have eaten.
We should have sung songs.	We could have studied.	We must have driven too far.	We might have driven too far.
They should have sat in class.	They could have read.	They must have grown up.	They might have walked home.

Passive Modals	Present Passive	Past Passive	Future Passive
Put the direct object in subject position. Follow it with a modal, the base form of *be*, and the past participle of the verb.	Put the direct object in subject position. Follow it with the present of *be* and the past participle of the verb.	Put the direct object in subject position. Follow it with the past of *be* and the past participle of the verb.	Put the direct object in subject position. Follow it with the (modal) future marker *will*, the base form of *be*, and the past participle of the verb.
Bottles can be recycled. Women will be honored. Bob might be hired. Books should be read. English must be taught.. Songs could be sung.	That book is always read. His movies are rarely watched.	The food was eaten. The cars were driven safely.	The can will be opened. All languages will be spoken.

Tense Forms

Present Real Conditional	Present Unreal Conditional	Passt Unreal Conditional
Use *if* and the present tense of the verb in the *if clause*, and the future (*will* or *be going to*) and the base form of the verb in the main clause. (*Might* can be used for a weaker result.)	Use *if* and the past tense of the verb in the *if clause*, and *would* followed by the base form of the verb in the main clause.	Use *if* and the past perfect tense of the verb in the *if clause* and *would have*, followed by the past participle of the verb, in the main clause.
If I speak English well, I will apply for a better job. If I speak English well, I am going to apply for a better job.	If I spoke English well, I would apply for a better job.	If I had spoken English well, I would have applied for a better job.
If you work hard, you will get a raise.	If you worked hard, you would get a raise.	If you had worked hard, you would have gotten a raise.
If it eats too much, it will gain weight.	If it ate too much it would gain weight.	If it had eaten too much, it would have gained weight.
If we study hard we are going to pass the test.	If we studied hard, we would pass the test.	If we had studied hard, we would have passed the test.
If they read the book, they will learn something new.	If they read the book, they would learn something new.	If they had read the book, they would have learned something new.

When *if clauses* are reversed, no comma is needed.

It will gain weight if it eats too much.
It would gain weight if it ate too much.
It would have gained weight if it had eaten too much.

Index

The number indicates the page where the word or phrase first appears in this *Teacher's Manual*.